Have Yourself a Stressless Little Christmas

Darla Satterfield Davis

WHITE STONE BOOKS
LAKELAND, FLORIDA

08 07 06 05   10 9 8 7 6 5 4 3 2 1

Have Yourself a Stressless Little Christmas
ISBN 1-59379-026-0
Copyright © 2005 Darla Satterfield Davis

Published by White Stone Books, Inc.
P.O. Box 2835
Lakeland, Florida 33806

Dedication

For my parents
Donald and Laverna Satterfield
and our family...
may we be an unbroken circle in Heaven one day,
celebrating the greatest Christmas ever!

Introduction

Let me ask you a question, "Do you remember what Grandma, Aunt Rita, or cousin Scott got you for Christmas last year? Probably not, but if you are like me, I bet you remember very well the warm hugs and the welcoming smiles you drove all that way to see.

Let's face it, folks, the truth is by the time Christmas melts into spring we have long forgotten most of the details we so meticulously planned for the Christmas holidays. The real memories that hold us are not the details, but the love, warmth, and good times we shared with our families and loved ones.

To be honest, most toddlers will have as much fun playing with the box their toys came in as the toy itself! It's their giggles and smiles; the pictures with proud grandparents; the lipstick smudges on their cheeks—that we look lovingly back on when we remember the holidays.

Christmas shouldn't be so much about what you have, or how everything looked--as who was there and what you did to share those moments and make them special.

This Christmas try letting go of the perfectionism that drives us to a place of guilt and robs our joy in the season. Let's instead consider "doing" less and "experiencing" more with our families and loved ones. Let's worry less about how it "looks" and what we spend, and more on how it "feels" and what will be remembered.

This year let's make more memories and make all the moments count!

Darla Satterfield Davis

Contents

CREATIVE CHRISTMAS CRAFTS

COOKIN' UP CHRISTMAS!

LET'S GO CAROLING

ABOUT THE AUTHOR

Be Prepared!

THE EMERGENCY CHRISTMAS KIT

A MUST HAVE!

What do you do when an unexpected guest shows up on your front doorstep? With your handy Emergency Christmas Kit and these easy steps, you can be prepared like the pros.

Get a box, preferably a large shoe or hat box, that has a lid. It can be decorated or wrapped to match the Christmas theme you have selected for your home.

Fill the box with the following items:

* Christmas napkins
* 2-scented votive candles
* 2-wine goblets
* A box of matches
* A Christmas CD
* Cinnamon sticks
* Ground cinnamon
* Hot chocolate packets
* Christmas ornaments and be sure to include your family name with the year.

Items to keep refrigerated:

❄ Butter

❄ Frozen muffins

When a guest shows up unexpectedly simply follow these easy steps to make your home appeal to the senses and your company feel warm and appreciated.

🎅 Put the votives in the goblets and light them for a soft glow.

🎅 Turn on your Christmas CD to create a nostalgic atmosphere.

🎅 Put the cinnamon sticks in a pan with water and simmer on the stove for a fantastic fragrance.

🎅 Take out some muffins and microwave them for a few minutes. Spread butter and sprinkle cinnamon on top when warm. Set on a napkin and serve.

🎅 Heat up some hot chocolate.

🎅 Give your guest a Christmas ornament for his or her tree.

WHEN WEATHER STRIKES!

You never know when a weather-related mishap will occur. It's a good idea to keep the following items on hand at home as well as in your car when traveling.

At Home:

 Keep rock salt handy for driveways and walkways.

 Store bottled water.

Keep extra blankets on hand in case the heat goes out.

Matches and candles are good for power outages.

Flashlights and batteries

Beanie wienies, trail mix, pudding packs. Stock your pantry with canned goods and foods that do not need to be cooked if your house is all electric.

Keep your cell phone charged.

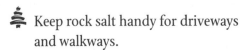

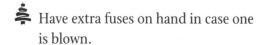 Battery-operated radios are great to find out about the conditions outside.

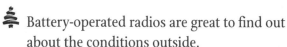 Have extra fuses on hand in case one is blown.

In the Car:

 Keep rock salt handy for driveways.

Keep kitty litter in the trunk—it adds weight and traction if you get stuck.

 Keep bottled water in your trunk for emergencies.

Extra blankets provide warmth when needed.

 Keep flashlights and batteries in case your car breaks down at night.

 Keep de-icers and scrapers in your car for those icy days.

 Keep your cell phone charged in case of emergency.

14

Time-savers
& Tips

TIMESAVING SHORTCUTS

Try some of these time-savers to help put the zip back in your doo-dah!

- Gift bags save time and can be purchased at discount and dollar stores for half the department store prices...or less!

- Paying a teenager or a neighbor who doesn't work to do your gift wrapping is also a quick, easy option and a great way to hide your presents. Hand it over and don't look back!

- Frozen foods and entrées are amazingly good these days. Check out your grocer's frozen food section and see what appeals to you. You can entertain well in minutes with a hot oven and some nice serving dishes.

- Visit your local deli. It can be a fast way to get tidbits on the table in a hurry. Watch your paper around holiday times and see what restaurants and stores are offering specials on deli trays and catering.

- Avoid the temptation to overcommit. Memorize this phrase: "Good idea! Maybe next year!" or "Sorry, I can't. Try me next year." Trust me, you'll thank yourself later.

🌿 Have your baked goods made by an elderly or retired individual, who would likely appreciate the additional funds for the holiday and would have great experience in the kitchen, as well. You can also have a teen help—but a little advice: Make sure your teen has eaten a BIG dinner before turning him or her loose with all those goodies!

🌿 Approach a teen at your church youth group to baby-sit for a little Christmas cash!

🌿 Here is a real time-saver if you start out early enough...like July...cook big pots of soup, chili, stew, or beans. Cool them and put them in freezer bags in family-size proportions. When you are out shopping or just come in and are too tired to prepare dinner, you can pull out your good homemade soups, add a salad and bread, and you are done!

🌿 Have a teen run your errands. This is especially exciting for new drivers. Keep in mind the holiday traffic...having these done as early in the day as feasible.

🌿 Keep the men in your life helping by having them make sure the car is gassed up and road ready at all times. They can carry in and haul stuff out too!

GIFT WRAP SHORTCUTS

🎄 Fastest wrapping in the West? Gift bags and tissue paper!

🎄 A decorated gift box with a stick on bow does it quick and neat.

🎄 Big or odd-shaped object? Wrap in white trash bags and tie with a big fluffy red bow!

🎄 Out of Christmas paper? Wrap in white or tissue paper and spruce it up with a real ribbon or a lace bow.

🎄 How about using the comics out of the newspaper? Kids love them!

🎄 Place baked goodies in a clear canister and tie with a pretty bow.

🎄 Try a solid paper of any kind and add stickers, stamps, or glitter spray!

🎄 Wrap goodies in a colored, holiday-printed cellophane.

🎄 Dress up an average package by adding a sprig of silk holly.

🎄 Use snowflake garland from the dollar store. Cut and use on your packages in place of ribbon.

🎄 Put your gift in a holiday stocking and baste it shut with thread.

🎄 No gift box? Keep them guessing by using a cereal or cracker box to wrap your gift in!

DELEGATE DAHLING!—
HOW TO AND WHO TO!

Make a grocery list and send your hubby
or other family member shopping in
your place!

Make tree trimming a warm family affair!
With everyone helping, the tree will go up,
memories will be made, and your
decorating/cleaning time will be cut
in half.

Assign each family member a task for your
parties or get-togethers, one in charge of
punch and drinks, one for coats, and one for
garbage detail.

Have your children prepare for "their"
guests by readying their rooms and
planning for fun.

HOLIDAY CLEANUP TIPS

Buy paper and plastic dinnerware and THROW IT AWAY when you are done! Some are quite festive...all are a good investment for saving time!

Use zipper bags to store leftovers and goodies in. You can throw them away when finished.

Lay a clear plastic cover over your lace tablecloth for easy wiping and protecting your heirloom. A plastic drop cloth from the hardware section works great.

Heavy-duty bags are a good investment for the extra loads of garbage this time of year.

Line cookie sheets with wax paper for easy cleanup after baking.

Dinner baked in foil in the oven feeds a hungry group and keeps pots and pans clean and clear!

Use cooking spray on your casserole dishes before you bake anything for easier clean up.

Set a wastebasket beside you when you wrap presents and drop scraps in as you work.

Give each child a box to put their gifts in and a trash bag to put their wrappings in as they open their gifts. This cuts down on the mess and on many lost toys and pieces!

Limit Christmas festivities to one room and get everyone to help straighten up before they go play with their new toys.

Appoint a garbage detail unit to take care of all trash and haul it out!

FASTEST WRAPPING IN THE WEST! QUICK AND CREATIVE GIFT WRAPPING IDEAS

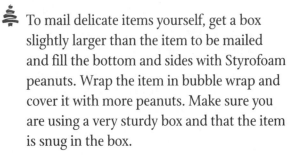 To mail delicate items yourself, get a box slightly larger than the item to be mailed and fill the bottom and sides with Styrofoam peanuts. Wrap the item in bubble wrap and cover it with more peanuts. Make sure you are using a very sturdy box and that the item is snug in the box.

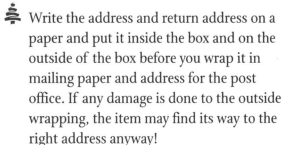 Write the address and return address on a paper and put it inside the box and on the outside of the box before you wrap it in mailing paper and address for the post office. If any damage is done to the outside wrapping, the item may find its way to the right address anyway!

Always use good strapping tape and plenty of it!

Make sure you use no-run ink when addressing your mail. Winter can be soggy out there!

Be sure you insure your boxes and, if you receive one that is damaged, do not throw any of the string, tape, or wrapping paper away as the postmaster will require you to bring it in for your claim.

When buying gifts that have to be mailed, think about size and weight as items can be very costly to send.

If you use stick-on return address labels on packages, tape them down so they won't peel off.

Most offices, schools, and stores have packaging materials they will give you for free if you ask early enough.

Print clearly ON ALL YOUR CORRESPONDENCE...especially this time of year!

Moneymakers
&
Money Savers

CHA-CHING!
A PENNY SAVED
IS A PENNY EARNED

Think of your gifts and talents. Maybe you are a great knitter and can make beautiful afghans for gifts, or your husband is great with vehicles and his gift could be used as a "car rescue coupon."

- Watch the mailers for special sales and coupons.
- Make it homemade—it doesn't have to come from a store. See pages 102-115 for easy and creative ideas.
- Homemade Coupons—ideas could be: baby-sitting for a young couple who doesn't get to go out much, car washing, or lawn services (these are great suggestions to help young people join in on the gift giving).
- Visit your local dollar store. You'd be surprised at the neat items you can find—especially for children.
- Take an item from your home that has been admired by someone else (a picture, jewelry, candlesticks, etc.) and give it to them with a note as to why it is sentimental to you.
- With today's technology, create personalized stationery or calendars.
- Prepare a box full of baked goodies.

CHRISTMAS IN JULY...
PLAN AHEAD FOR NEXT YEAR!

❄ Shop those after Christmas sales!

❄ Begin handmade items while you are resting from this year's chores.

❄ Order now from sales catalogs!

❄ Watch for store closeouts all year and stock up!

❄ Choose a closet or a locking cabinet to store next year's bounty.

❄ Do some early fact-finding about people you want to buy for next year.

❄ You can even wrap gifts ahead of time so you don't have to store wrapping paper, as long as you mark the gifts well!

❄ Buy holiday storage tins and canisters ahead of time so you are ready.

❄ Buy Christmas cards in January and have them addressed by Thanksgiving, ready to be mailed on December 1st.

❄ Keep an open Christmas letter or document on your computer; you can add tidbits throughout the year for a more interesting letter in December.

MONEYMAKING PROJECTS FOR KIDS

- Homemade Christmas cards to sell or send...Mom, you would buy their cards. What family member wouldn't appreciate a new artist in training?

- Gather mistletoe and tie ribbons on the sprigs to sell.

- Offer to gift wrap for others.

- Rake leaves or shovel snow.

- Offer to pet sit while others are away.

- Offer to clean a car or house for a family member or neighbor.

- Assist an adult with hanging Christmas decorations.

- Run errands (especially to the grocery store.)

- Make something homemade—see page 102.

- Baby-sit a younger sibling.

- If you know your neighbors well, you could make address labels for them on your computer and give them out early enough for holiday mailings. It's inexpensive and personal!

Life Savers

HOW TO REJUVENATE YOU AND STAY RELAXED DURING THE HOLIDAYS

- Save a little money for yourself and take a spa day, or at least get a facial or pedicure!

- Don't be afraid to stretch out now and then for a quick "power nap."

- If you are on the road, try scented towelettes for your face or temples and wrists...feels good, and the aroma therapy is a real pick-me-up.

- Try a new fragrant lotion and keep it on your desk for a quick hand massage and freshening up during your busy day.

- Make time to sit in a warm, candle-lit bath!

- Christmas or other calming music playing in your home or while you are at work opens the heart and calms the brain.

- Buy a variety of energy snacks to keep on hand. Nutrition is a great stress fighter!

- At lunch, stop at the park to eat and watch the winter wonderland outdoors. If it's cold, enjoy the change of scenery from your car.

- Just for fun...buy yourself a small gift, wrap it up, and put it under your tree.

- Don't cook tonight! Bring dinner home and spend the extra few minutes saved on you!

"HEALTHY NEW YEAR!" HOW TO SAIL INTO THE NEW YEAR HEALTHY AND HAPPY

🍪 ZZZZZ! Make sure you catch enough Z-Z-Zs even if you are busy! A good night's rest will help you work faster and more effectively.

🍪 Take extra vitamin C to fight off those cold and flu bugs!

🍪 If you are considered an "at risk" person, get that flu shot early!

🍪 Use LOTS or disinfectant lotion OFTEN... especially when you grocery shop with a cart!

🍪 Change linens and towels more often at home.

🍪 Open the window even for just a few minutes to let healthy fresh air in!

🍪 Don't put off or miss those doctor appointments even if it is a busy time. Your health is more important.

🍪 Brrr! Avoid moving the thermostat up and down, as constant changes in temperature can cause colds and sniffles.

🍪 Use those antibacterial towelettes on phone receivers and high traffic areas.

🍪 Keep lip balm and hand lotion with you at all times.

Deck the Halls
Ya'll!

FUN CHRISTMAS
DECORATING
THEMES

CREATING A CUBICAL CHRISTMAS

Lack of space...no need to miss the holidays! Any one or all of these festive ideas will make the workplace fun!

- Edge your cubical with garland, mini lights, or holly. A touch of festive color without it getting in the way!

- Hats! Save space and have a JOLLY time with your coworkers by investing in a variety of fun holiday hats. Santa caps, crazy hats, a tiara, it doesn't matter. Have fun! If it's on your head—it isn't in the way of your elbows.

- The top of your computer screen is a great place for a tiny tree.

- Decorate a sign and place it on the back of your chair to give your coworkers a giggle.

- You can even "entertain" during breaks at your cubicle by keeping small stacking canisters of goodies on hand.

- If you are out of space "in" your cubicle, try hanging decorations above it.

A Christmassy little throw rug or even a dish of fragrant potpourri can add a touch of the season to your little corner of the world.

There's always room for bows! Even in small spaces bright red Christmas bows are just the ticket.

The coffee area is a great place to spread a little holiday cheer. Bring some special flavored coffees and creamers for the holiday season. Take turns bringing "goodies" for break time. Decorate the area with colored napkins and holiday coffee cups. Don't forget a few packets of spiced cider and hot chocolate to add some fun flavor to your break!

Don't forget to decorate YOU! Wearing beautiful or funny accessories during the Christmas season breaks up the monotony of everyday life in a cubicle.

Place wreaths around your office...don't forget the bathroom doors!

Put Christmas pictures or posters over the ones on your desk or in the office. A change of scenery can be nice.

A CARDINAL CHRISTMAS

🎄 Use small red lights.

🎄 Tie red bows on the branches.

🎄 Use red berry garland.

🎄 Make a large red bow for the top of the tree that leaves five or so streamers hanging down around the tree.

🎄 Place red cardinals/red birds on the branches.

🎄 Place fake snow in clumps on the ends of the branches.

🎄 Use garland, red lights, and cardinals along the top of the fireplace mantle and also on the center of your dining room table.

🎄 The addition of red candle tapers can make a stunning statement.

🎄 Red bows on the napkins and glasses make a nice touch.

CLASSIC CHRISTMAS

- Use red and green ribbon. (If you watch your craft and hobby stores, you can find great discount deals.)

- Tie red bows on several branches.

- Make a large bow for the top of the tree that leaves five streamers hanging down around the tree.

- Use the same type of ribbon and make large bows to pull back your curtains.

- Ribbon streamers can also be used along an entertainment system, coffee table, or bookshelf to add a festive look and tie in your color theme.

ANGELIC CHRISTMAS

🎀 White lights. (As many as possible!)

🎀 Stretch angel hair over the branches and lights. (Be sure to wear rubber gloves since angel hair is actually long strands of spun glass.) It reflects light beautifully when stretched over a tree and the effect is magnificent!

🎀 Place white ornaments and/or angel figurines in garland stretched across a fireplace and on a dining room table.

🎀 Spread the theme throughout the rest of your house by using white ribbon, candles, and white figurines or ornaments to decorate tables, bookshelves, or walls.

🎀 Hang snowflakes above the table and anywhere else appropriate.

TOYLAND CHRISTMAS

These decorations are very inexpensive yet tons of fun. Especially enjoyable when small children are around. Not only easy to put together, but festive, colorful, and for all practical purposes can be done with little to no money.

- Raid your children's bedrooms of all the stuffed animals you can find. (We recommend you do this while they are at school.)

- You can make paper chains for garland. (Children love to help make these!)

- Fill your tree, wreaths, and garland with stuffed animals. (You can involve young children in this activity since there are no breakables involved.)

- To create a color theme, add bows to all the animals. (This is also a great way to continue a color theme throughout your home.)

- Hang Santa hats on the walls and doors with a few toys peeking out the top. (This is a great decoration especially for children's bedroom doors.)

- If you have an electric train or car set, place it under the tree for a festive look.

- Polish off the tree, wreaths, and other decorations by adding candy canes.

- Hang candy canes all over the tree.

CHRISTMAS ON THE RANGE

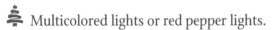

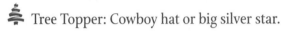

- Multicolored lights or red pepper lights.

- Tree Topper: Cowboy hat or big silver star.

- For garland use thin rope or metallic silver garland with stars.

- Use a quilt or Mexican blanket for your tree skirt.

- Fill tree with ornaments such as: toy-sized cowboy boots, metal stars, toy horses, and small cowboy hats.

- Be creative and have fun! You could also use stick peppermint wrapped with twine and small toy farm animals, or black and white cows.

- As a fun gift wrapping idea use brown boxing paper with red ribbons...accent with red bandanas, which can be purchased at any craft store. Also, use red paper with raffia tied around the packages.

Place cowboy boots by the fireplace and around the house filled with pine greenery.

 Use red bandanas to accent your tree, packages, table settings, etc. (You can make a bandana bow very easily by folding it in half and gathering it in the middle, securing it with a rubber band tightly around the middle, then fluffing!)

 For a great table setting use a quilt or Mexican blanket for the tablecloth, red bandanas for placemats, canning jars for glasses. Place a cowboy hat in the middle and bright red berries about the table. Place cinnamon sticks tied with red ribbon or raffia at each place setting.

SNOWMEN ON PARADE!

❄ Use colors of blue and silver.

❄ Small white or blue lights

❄ Blue metallic and/or snowflake garland

❄ Hang snowmen ornaments along with blue and silver balls.

❄ Silver jingle bells add a nice touch as well.

❄ Hang snowflakes on tree branches and everywhere else!

❄ Adding shimmering icicles that can be scattered all over will add dimension and sparkle to your exciting tree!

❄ Use blue and silver papers, plain and patterned. Use with blue and silver ribbons of various sizes. You can make extra snowmen and tie on your packages or simply add a big silver snowflake to carry on your theme.

Gift Giving

NOEL NO-NOS—FOR WOMEN:

- Blenders, vacuums, toasters, and the like. Even if she "needs" them, she'll appreciate something more personal.

- Perfume or clothing like your "mother used to wear."

- T-shirts you may think are humorous referring to any part of her anatomy, for any reason.

- Gardening tools or sports equipment that happens to be in YOUR line of activity not hers. Are you picking up the hints here?

- Anything you secretly want for yourself and think she won't realize. She will realize it!

- Products that remove unwanted hair, wrinkles, cellulite, or may "enhance" the figure. Just don't go there.

NOEL DOS—FOR WOMEN:

- Themed gift baskets (relaxation basket containing: a soothing CD, bath salts, scented body lotions, aromatherapy candles, etc.) See page 54 for ideas.

- Sentimental jewelry. Diamonds are always a safe bet.

- Tickets to a play or ballet and a promise of a romantic dinner.

- A gift card to her favorite clothing store

- A book she would enjoy with a personal inscription from you.

- Coupons for a weekend getaway to a bed and breakfast

- A year's subscription to her favorite magazine

- Find out what her hobbies are and get a tool or items she might not buy for herself.

- A mother's ring or pin makes a lovely gift.

- Photo albums, family portraits, and heartfelt notes and letters will win her heart every time!

- What your lady really wants is your heart! Buy her a small sentimental gift and take the time to write her a long love letter telling her why she is the only woman in the world for you!

- Just a little insider tip here: Give her your ear, and she will likely TELL you what she really wants!

NOEL NO-NOS—FOR MEN:

 Clappers. (You know, to turn on and off the lights.)

 Anything "just like your father used to wear."

 Any sports jersey that you will get tired of seeing him in EVERY weekend until it wears out!

 Anything that may promote or encourage a bad habit you want him to quit.

 Kits or "Do it Yourself" books— like how to build your own airplane, hang glider, motorcycle, or anything else that might cause you undue stress.

 Anything that causes an aroma you would not like in your home. Modeling glue, plastic tennis shoes...you get the picture.

 No matter HOW tempted you are...resist all anti-snoring devices.

 Gag gifts that pertain to his imperfections...hair restorers, nose clippers, hats with unflattering comments, T-shirts that point out the already obvious flaw

 Colognes that his mom used to buy him when he was twelve

 Mystery colognes that are in bottles you think look cool.

 No more socks! Especially no more brown socks!

NOEL DOS—FOR MEN:

- A voice activated remote. (We just couldn't resist adding this one!)
- A leather portfolio
- Grilling tool kit
- Paper shredder
- Ipod
- Digital camera
- Magazine subscriptions to his favorite interest or hobby
- A wireless headset
- Music CDs of his favorite groups
- Books by his favorite author.
- Sports equipment related to his passion or interests
- Tool time! Women don't, but guys **do** want tools for Christmas...go figure!
- Golf lessons are available at country clubs and golf courses everywhere.
- Men are still boys at heart and generally love an adventure. How about a skydiving session, snorkeling class, formula car racing for a day? Hot air balloon, hang gliding session...set of thrill seekers movies? It just depends on how adventurous your man is!
- Personalized desk sets that reflect his interests

NOEL NO-NOS—FOR TEENS:

 Colorful permanent hair dye

 Anything marked with an explosion warning on the label

 Clothes with words or slogans you do not personally understand

 Tickets to concerts where bands have names that might scare or confuse you

 Anything for a guy that you picked up and thought, *Isn't that cute?*

 Anything for a girl that you picked up and thought, *Hey I used to wear one of these when I was her age!*

NOEL DOS—FOR TEENS:

- Pre-paid movie tickets

- Concert tickets

- Pre-paid Visa cards

- Gift certificates to favorite stores that encourage a hobby or talent

- Pre-paid gas cards

- Certificates offering privileges, such as curfew extensions, use of the new car Dad bought, or a messy room bypass, etc.

- Digital or disposable cameras

- Ipods

- A basket of snacks and a gift card to the local movie rental establishment for a night of snacks and entertainment

- Techno toys

- Palm pilot

- Software upgrades

- Cash

NOEL NO-NOS—FOR KIDS:

- Anything with more than ten pieces

- Things that could cause wounds in the middle of the night

- Duracell Energizer bunnies

- Toys marked "Adult Supervision Required"

- Any item that states an instruction book is enclosed

- Anything marked "ink included"

- Anything marked "live" on the box

- Anything that has eyes that "glow in the dark"

- Any object that you can hear with the bedroom door closed or across the street

- Anything that amplifies a voice or instrument

- Anything marked "Assembly Required."

NOEL DOS—FOR KIDS:

- Holiday shirts for decorating.
- Modeling clay and cookie cutters to celebrate the season.
- Collect old Christmas cards and give to a child to create a collage of their own for the holiday. Provide the poster so they can put it up in their room.
- Disposable cameras
- Stickers
- Light up pens or cool, decorative pencils
- Erasable marker kits
- Colorful plastic straw cups and straw bowls to eat/drink from
- Waterproof, colorful table placemats
- Favorite character throw pillows
- A special kid's blanket
- Bean bag chairs
- Snow Cone Machine (good anytime of year).
- Bath Bubbles, Soap, and/or Foam
- Subscription to *Highlights* magazine or interest magazines on subjects like spiders, nature, science, motorbikes, trains, or collectible dolls.
- Science kits, telescopes, building models. Keep it age appropriate and in an area they are currently interested in!
- Sports equipment and toys for them to play with outdoors, such as balls, bats, rackets, and more
- Skates, ice skates, roller blades, or skateboards. Get them and the safety gear and watch your kids get into healthy habits while they are young.

BIG FAMILY SMALL BUDGET—GIFT GIVING FOR A LARGE FAMILY

- Games! Get a game, or even a game set for the family to share!

- A basket of fruit and goodies never goes to waste in a big family.

- Snack Canisters. Give each member a different small canister with his or her favorite snack inside. They can mix and match, share, and refill!

- Ice cream for everyone! An ice-cream coupon for each family member is an inexpensive and fun gift idea.

- Fill a basket with video rental coupons, popcorn, and candies.

- A family movie video

- A music CD the whole family will enjoy

- A computer game all can share

- Large cookies with each family member's name iced on it

WHAT TO GET GRANDMA OR THOSE WITH LIMITED LIVING SPACE

- Good Eatin'! Give gift cards for restaurants in their area. Make it for two so a friend can be invited. No one likes dining out alone!

- Pay the paperboy! A year subscription to the paper leaves more change in Grandpa's jeans!

- Motorcycle magazine subscription? Well, not every grandparent gardens you know!

- Count Basey and his band never sounded as good as he does on a new CD! And while you are at it...why not a new CD player!

- John Wayne is still bigger than life on VHS and DVD! A new copy might be fun.

- Books on tape or CD make great gifts for those who tire easily when reading.

- One friend I know had grandparents who lived way out in the country where cable wasn't available...so over the year they recorded hours and hours of their grandparent's favorite game shows and movies. They were thrilled!

- "A night on the town." A coupon good for an evening out with your loved one. They really want your time most of all anyway!

- Bringing bright and cheery pillows, stuffed animals, socks, and flowers can always brighten a person's day. Maybe Grandma NEEDS a "Sponge Bob" pillow on her bed!

AFFORDABLE GIFTS FOR COWORKERS

❄ Scented candles

❄ Stretch gloves

❄ Ice scrapers

❄ Guest soaps or bath beads

❄ Ornaments

❄ Scented items for the car

❄ Nail polish

❄ Fun writing tablet

❄ Ink pens

❄ Holiday pins

❄ Flashlights

❄ Candies

❄ Packages of cocoa or hot cider with a mug

❄ Fish hooks, golf balls, and hobby-related items are always a hit.

❄ "Silent Night" is a fun game to play with your coworkers. You can buy small gifts and wrap them at home. Each night before you leave, put an unmarked gift on a different person's desk. The joy of giving is not limited to big gifts; small surprises from an unknown source bring joy to all!

GIFTS FOR BABY'S FIRST CHRISTMAS

- Buy a journal and pass it around the family having them each write notes, prayers, or poems. Each member should date and sign his or her entry.

- Purchase an engraved ornament, a hand-painted one, or even make a homemade ornament with the child's name and the date on it.

- Start a tradition of buying this child a special ornament each year with the date on it.

- Look for picture frames that will fit the new baby's birth announcement.

- A Bible with baby's full name engraved on the cover

- A baby quilt with the child's name and information embroidered on it

- Special Christmas place setting for baby

- Any engraved item with the year included

- A framed copy of the family tree with baby's name added

- If you have time to obtain the mother and father's baby pictures—you could include all three photos in a combination frame. It is sometimes uncanny how similar parents and their babies look, and who wouldn't treasure such a gift.

FAMILY HEIRLOOMS AS GIFTS

A special item your loved one has always admired might be a nice gift to pass down. Be sure the dates and information are on all items you wish to pass on to family members so the story and family history continues.

These might include:

 Handmade quilts.

 Hand embroidered pillowcases are wonderful to pass down.

 Music boxes, figurines, photo albums, a family Bible, silverware, china, artwork, hankies, gloves, hats, clocks and time pieces, jewelry, and sports equipment like guns or knives, but only to the right family member!

 I once had a friend whose aunt took a beautiful old tablecloth that had been intricately embroidered by a great-great-grandmother. The fabric in certain places was soiled, but by cutting out sections and framing them, these pieces became treasured gifts that Christmas for several daughters, granddaughters, cousins, and nieces. On the back of each piece was a note explaining who the embroidered piece came from and that it had been embroidered in her first year of marriage during a passage from Holland to the United States.

"SENTIMENTAL ME" GIFTS— MAKE IT PERSONAL

- Choose a book that will be meaningful to them and write a personal inscription in it...and the date!

- Print personalized stationary on your computer and include their name in the artwork.

- Have a personalized license plate made.

- Embroidered pillowcases with the family name or monogram are a nice touch.

- A special Christmas ornament with signature and date

- Try a doormat with the family name.

- Make a greeting sign for the home with the family's name on it.

- Make or buy personalized key chains.

- A decorated bulletin board with the name painted across the top is a great gift for kids and teens.

- How about a hand-painted or stenciled mailbox

- Pen and pencil set with name engraved

- Personalized coffee mugs or goblets

- A picture frame with a portrait of you and the recipient

- Personalized car mats—guys love them!

GREAT GIFT BASKET IDEAS

Pamper Me: Fill with bubble bath, lotions, potpourri, votive or tea candles, a CD, and a card expressing your thanks and appreciation. List specific items or memories if you can.

The Newlyweds: Fill with two stemmed goblets, sparkling grape juice, a soft music CD, chocolates, candles, real or silk rose petals, and a small photo album. Include a card with well wishes.

Family Fun Night!: Fill with a movie and/or movie rental coupons, popcorn, a puzzle and/or game set, and miscellaneous snacks.

Celebrate Christmas: Fill with hot cocoa and/or cider mix, festive mugs, soup mixes, a Christmas CD, Christmas candies or cookies, and this book! Don't forget the Christmas card.

Class Act Teacher: Fill with coupons for a manicure, fun note pads and stationery, a Christmas ornament, a nice pen, and be sure to enclose a note of thanks.

The New Baby Basket: Fill with a soft blanket, diapers, a stuffed animal, a store gift card, a picture frame, a baby's first Christmas ornament, a baby music CD, and bibs or any special engraved item.

Here's to the Cook: Fill a basket with fun cookie cutters of all types, cookie mixes, and different types of sprinkles and decorations. Mix in a cookbook, too!

A LIVING GIFT OF FAMILY HISTORY

Start a family history book. It is best to begin with a 3-ring binder. There are family stories only you know from your perspective. They can become valued keepsakes to others. Now isn't the time to reveal family secrets though! If you need a starting place, write down funny memories of when family members were younger, or possibly fond memories you frequently recall of someone else. If you have pictures you can include them. It's not about being perfect, it's about creating a lasting family treasure. By using a 3-ring binder, others can begin to participate and make additions to your notebook and copies can be made for others. You can begin a meaningful tradition by bringing your notebook each year to the family Christmas gathering.

There are many websites you can visit to research your family history. Many have printable family trees, crests, and other useful information. Visit these sites for more information:

www. familytreemaker.com

www.genealogy.com

www.familytreesearcher.com

CHRISTMAS FOR SHUT-INS

 Send a care package with treats and gifts.

 Write an anonymous letter to a shut-in describing a great time the two of you had together and have him or her "Guess Who" wrote the letter. Send the answer and another story the next day!

 "Partners in Crime." Don't forget to include a shut-in's roommate or even a pet when you bring goodies or plan a visit. It will brighten Fido's day too!

 You are still blue? Get dressed up, buy some small gifts, and head to the children's ward at a hospital and spread a little joy!

 Sing carols (refer to pages 134) in a hospital or nursing home and hand out candy canes or Christmas cards.

 Offer to decorate a central visiting area of a nursing home facility or hospital.

 Organize a team at your church—possibly with the youth group—and create your own angel tree for church members that are unable to get out.

FELIZ DE FIDO!
CELEBRATE THE PET!

Gifts for Pets:

- A new chew toy will keep Bowser barking.

- A cat nip toy for Miss Kitty

- If you live in a cold climate a doggie sweater can make "Snuggles" live up to his name.

- Special doggie or kitty treats are nice for your pet. You could even feed them holiday sweets from your table. It is, after all, Christmas!

- Does your family need a new buddy? If you are home for the holidays and have some time off, this could be a good time to bring in a new pet and start the training process. Choose wisely!

- If your pet has neighborhood "friends" a little gift bag with a chew toy, a ball, and some doggie biscuits is a fun way to share the holiday with your neighbor and their pet. For Miss Kitty's friends include a fuzzy mouse filled with cat nip, a can of kitty treats, and a feather toy.

- The best gift you could give your pet for Christmas is a care and training book for YOU!

SEASON'S GREETINGS FOR CLERGY, TEACHERS, MAILMEN, PAPERBOYS, MANICURISTS, AND OTHERS

❄ Books on a favorite topic or about their area of expertise

❄ Gift certificates are great...even for small amounts

❄ Pen and pencil sets

❄ Calculator

❄ Personalized note pads

❄ Special candies

❄ Cheese/meat assortment boxes

❄ Name plates

❄ Framed Bible verse

❄ Funny sticky notes

SMALL GIFTS KIDS CAN EXCHANGE

Teaching our children how to give is an important life lesson! Help them learn by giving!

- If your child is like mine was and wanted to give something to EVERYONE she knew, consider party bags with a cookie, small toy, and a Christmas Bible verse. You can find very affordable items at dollar shops.

- Tie 'em up! Friendship bracelets are a good gift that are inexpensive to buy and less expensive to make!

- Never underestimate the power of the old standby—the candy cane! Include the story of the candy cane with each one; it is a great story and a sweet gift. (See page 105 for the story.)

- A small stocking with their name in glitter still seems to be one of the favorites for kids. Fill with tiny treats and remember to visit the dollar store!

- Posters for their bedrooms are inexpensive and good gifts between friends. Have your little darling design one on the computer and save even more!

- T-shirts. There are always sales on T-shirts and sweatshirts at this time of the year. Go ahead and get your 3 for $10.00 special and let your children create Christmas scenes with fabric paints.

- Let your children color or paint blank paper table placemats (available at any paper supply store). If you have time, have them laminated. This is excellent as a gift for family members, especially if the name of the recipient is included.

CREATIVE WAYS TO GIVE MONEY AS A GIFT

Tape money end to end, and fanfold into a gift box with a pull-out tab slot. When the receiver pulls the tab, money keeps unfolding out!

Fold bills and make them into a ring or a bracelet.

Origami fold bills into all kinds of shapes for gifts...even a bouquet of paper money roses!

Leave hints around the house and have your recipient "treasure hunt" for the cash!

Fold bill or bills small and wrap inside box after box. Make them work for their dough!

Make a "green" wreath and present it to a family or couple.

Make a money tree...or Christmas tree.

Give a book with money slipped in between the pages...maybe at key points in the book or Bible.

Fill a helium balloon and float dollars inside!

Sew a bag and fill it with video game quarters or tokens.

AN ANGEL UNAWARE—WAYS TO GIVE ANONYMOUSLY!

 Send an unsigned Money Order. Leave off the return address or drop it off when they are not home! Make sure you leave it in a secure place—such as a mailbox door slot so that it cannot be stolen.

 Have your pastor or a person you can trust with your sweet secret deliver your gift for you.

 Send gift cards to stores. Do not include your name on the card.

 Order up! Order from a catalog and make sure that you are billed at your home and no packing slip is included in the box.

 Make a donation to a favorite charity and do it in memory of a loved one.

 Knock and run! Leave gifts on the porch, ring the bell, and hide! Make sure they are home first, of course!

 Take anonymous gifts to school and let the counselor deliver to your kids for you!

🎄 Hide and Seek—Leave little gifts and cards in places where family members will find them but not suspect you...at work, school, on their car window.

🎄 In shock! Go pay an electric or utility bill for a young family who is on a tight budget. Ask to remain anonymous!

🎄 Pin a gift or card or envelope on the company bulletin board with your friend's name on it.

🎄 Go to the bank, speak quietly to the teller, and ask to make a deposit in someone's account. Withdrawals they won't do; deposits they will! Ask them to keep your secret.

🎄 Have your gift delivered at a favorite restaurant, or have the bill pre-paid.

🎄 Sweet smell of Christmas—Send flowers anonymously. Or, why not a mini Christmas tree.

🎄 Fun for all—many service people will help you out with your secret gift and love to be in on the fun. Pay a manicurist for an extra manicure or pedicure. The paperboy, lawn specialists, and mechanics are all likely to help out.

IT'S THE NEIGHBORLY THING TO DO, YOU KNOW!

HOW TO INCLUDE A FRIEND WHO MAY BE ALONE THIS SEASON

🎄 The obvious answer here is to INCLUDE your friends in your activities.

🎄 Ask them out on a Christmas shopping trip.

🎄 Invite them to help you wrap presents and listen to Christmas songs.

🎄 This is a perfect time to invite them to your church for festivities.

🎄 Ask them to help you deliver food baskets to the needy. It is important to focus out!

🎄 Take time to listen! Let them tell you what they need!

🎄 Why not adopt a new member into your family festivities this Christmas.

WARM TIDINGS FOR NEIGHBORS

This is a time when it really is "the thought that counts" so much more than the gift. People don't interact as much as they used to. Be a trendsetter on your block!

- Offer to feed and water your neighbor's pets if they are going out of town and you are staying at home anyway!

- Taking the mail and picking up the newspapers for out-of-towners in your neighborhood will help keep their home safer, and yours too!

- A small Christmas book with poems or seasonal ideas might make a good gift for your special neighbors. (Hey! Maybe you could give them a book like, oh, say...this one!!)

- Carol from house to house and hand out a small card and a plate of goodies to a few neighbors.

- Want to make a neighbor a friend for life? Try offering to baby sit for them so they can have a night out for shopping without the kids in tow.

Who doesn't love the old Christmas movies,
especially the one about the Red Rider B.B. Gun!
How fun would it be to invite neighbors over to
watch it with you and drink a little hot cocoa
too? Just gather up the pillows and blankets,
and turn down the lights.

A giant candy cane in your yard with your street
name saying, "Merry Christmas Elm Street!"
sends a message to your neighbors without
having to entertain.

One of my favorite ways to remember my
neighbors is to write a personal note thanking
them for their neighborly deeds throughout the
year. I have some special neighbors whose
kindnesses have taught me so much about how
to be a good neighbor!

Time to Party!

GREAT ESCAPES

Excuses to leave a party early—some of them are pretty realistic sounding!

 The classic "I have a headache"...for tougher hosts try "Migraine."

My dog just had puppies and I need to go check on them.

My family called and is coming in unexpectedly, and I am not exactly sure when they will arrive.

I am sure I left a candle burning, and that silly cat is in the house.

We left the teenagers at home alone!

We just received a call from the babysitter, and I need to get home.

My cell phone is dead, and I am expecting a very important call.

I have a slow leak in my tire, and if I stay any longer I may not be able to make it to the service station to have it filled.

My schedule is very hectic right now, and I have another engagement I am expected at this evening.

The police warned me not to go off and leave my barbeque unattended...and besides, I am pretty sure all those leaves I stuffed in there have burned up by now. (Just Kidding!)

GREAT GIFT EXCHANGE IDEAS

Ornament Exchanges
Tie a bow and tag from the giver with the date; this can be enjoyed for future years while decorating the tree.

Books
Write on the first page why the book is important or meaningful to you. Draw names to exchange with, and each person reads why the book they received is meaningful.

Recipes
Bring a favorite dish with multiple recipe cards printed to exchange.

Story Item
Pick an item to exchange each year (like a yard gnome) and each year the recipient has to write a fictional story on where or what the item has done that past year. Include fake pictures or drawings if possible. This is especially nice for family parties.

Traditional "White Elephant Gift"
Bring an unwanted item from home. Draw numbers and take turns choosing a new gift or taking someone else's chosen item.

Christmas CDs
Bring a favorite Christmas CD and include a note as to why it is meaningful to you.

FUN PARTY FAVORS

Any of the items below would make a neat parting gift if a bow was added along with a written sentiment on a note or tag. Don't forget to add the year!

- Potpourri sachets

- Ornaments

- Mistletoe

- Small scented votives

- Christmas bells

- Angel or snowman figurines

- Small photo albums

- Chocolate or homemade sweets

- Your favorite Christmas recipe

SAY CHEESE! HOW TO TAKE FUN FAMILY PHOTOS DURING THE HOLIDAYS

🎄 Make sure you have extra film and batteries on hand.

🎄 Be creative and take some candid shots. Some of the best photos are those without a pose. Check out the area where the children are playing—or the kitchen...be sure to sneak a bite while you are there.

🎄 Don the antlers...why not?

🎄 If you'll be sending photos to members who are unable to attend, try preparing in advance a poster for the group to hold that reads, "Miss You, Grandma!"

🎄 Try to avoid pictures in front of windows or mirrors as they reflect.

🎄 If you take photos in front of the tree, make sure subjects are slightly to the side so it doesn't look as if objects are growing out of your heads!

🎄 Position group shots close together, making sure you can see each person clearly.

- Don't forget to turn on the "red eye" button on your camera if you are using a flash.

- If you are taking pictures prior to Christmas, make sure everyone has their holiday sweaters on.

- Make sure taller subjects are in the back or seated and shorter ones are in the front.

- Why not include your family pet in your shot? This may require a little patience.

- Those who wear glasses should tilt their heads slightly down so that the lenses don't glare in photos.

- Take several shots of each pose to make sure you get what you want.

- Shiny face or head? Use face powder before you take pictures.

- Check to make sure hair and clothing are in place, and ladies, don't forget that lip gloss.

- Why not strike a few crazy poses! Have some fun!

SMILE! YOU'RE ON CHRISTMAS CAMERA! HOW TO FILM YOUR CHRISTMAS EVENTS

❄ Recording with a video camera or digital camera can be fun. Try doing a little narration as you tape for more personalized memories.

❄ Film your kids doing their own play of the Nativity or Christmas Story.

❄ A family Christmas journal can keep your memories safe for generations to come. Write about each member of the family. Paste in pictures, wish lists, and even catalog pages with prices listed!

❄ Capsule! Fill a family time capsule and include pictures, news headlines, future predictions for each family member, prayers, and desires for the future. Seal it well, bury it, and wait 5 or 10 years. Be sure you bury it where it can be found again!

❄ Flash back! Arrange your family in a certain position or wearing Santa hats and take their picture every year in the same manner. In a few years, you will see how the kids have grown and the family changed.

❄ Put your old 8 mm films, tapes, and miscellaneous recordings together on CDs and make copies for each family member.

❄ Scan your old family photos and put them on discs to share or just to save.

Over the River and Through the Woods…to Grandmother's House We Go!

HOW TO PACK FOR YOUR TRIP

 Make a list of what you will need and keep it in a handy place. Add to it as thoughts come to mind.

 Choose "Mix and Match" outfits, keeping hues and colors the same so you can pack less.

 Make sure you pack medications, makeup, eye care, and other items you might need to frequently access in a carry-on case.

 As an extra precaution put nightwear and extra undies in your carry-on also! This is especially helpful when baggage is misplaced on a flight.

 A handy tip is to roll all your garments for packing. Less wrinkles—more room!

 Be sure to LEAVE ROOM for what you are bringing back from your trip!

 Miniaturize your toiletries in travel bottles and put in your flight bag.

Check the weather forecast and be prepared. These websites are great resources:

> www.weather.com
> www.cnn.com/WEATHER/
> http://weather.yahoo.com/

Make sure you pack all the shoes and accessories you will want to wear.

Use zipper bags to store jewelry, cosmetics, and small items you want to pack. Double zipper bag pump sprays.

Be sure to pack the following items...you'll be glad you did: disinfectant spray, scented candles and matches, extra nylons, handi-wipes, lotion, lip balm, and extra meds for stomach, headache, and other common discomforts.

Send packages and gifts ahead in large boxes. You don't have to send them overnight. Affordable methods will work just fine...as long as you allow plenty of time and BE SURE YOU USE A TRACEABLE METHOD!

BEFORE YOU LEAVE THE HOUSE, CHECK OFF YOUR LIST!

HOW TO BE A GOOD GUEST!

- Keep your things together and localized.
- Be polite and use "Please" and "Thank You" when making requests.
- Always ask before borrowing an item that doesn't belong to you.
- It's best to not bring a pet to someone else's house, but if you are unable to provide other arrangements for your animal, be sure you give advance notice and make certain it is not a nuisance to your host.
- Be helpful with household chores—take out the trash as soon as you see it getting full, offer to help with cooking and cleanup.
- Keep noise levels down.
- Write thank you notes for the hospitality given!
- Upon departure, strip the beds and offer to remake them.
- Leave the room you stay in as nice as you found it...every day of your stay.
- Keep as much as possible of your un-needed items packed away during your stay.
- Don't take over the host's favorite chair in the living room.
- Be courteous and follow the basic house rules and bedtimes.

COMPANY IS COMING!—HOW TO PREPARE FOR GUESTS

  Stock up on paper goods, especially toilet paper!

 Make sure all beds have fresh linens.

 Get an air bed if you need more places to sleep guests. Also, in a pinch, pool air mattresses work great, and kids love them.

 Check your supply of soaps, shampoo, and it doesn't hurt to buy an extra toothbrush or two.

 Stock up on soft drinks and juices.

 Make sure you have enough pillows.

 A night-light is appreciated in halls and bathrooms.

 Stock your cabinets and freezer so you don't have to shop after guests arrive.

 Gather brochures for local sites and events.

 Stock up on videos, games, and coloring books if children will be coming.

Find out if guests are bringing a pet and make accommodations.

 A welcome note on a pillow is always a nice touch.

TABLE SETTING TIPS AND HOW TO SEAT EXTRA GUESTS

- For big dinners, up with a centerpiece, napkins, and silverware but stack the plates on the kitchen and serve buffet style to save room for guests at the table.

- Add extra room by putting up a card table in the dining area.

- Seat children or teens at their own table in the same room or even in another room if they choose.

- A piece of plywood covered by a cloth enlarges your dining space. Be sure to place a folded sheet on top of your table before adding the plywood to keep it from scratching the surface. It will be important to keep the weight balanced on your table.

- Put a light blanket on top of the table before putting down your festive tablecloth. This will add a natural insulation for hot items.

- Move a small dining table aside and put up larger folding tables for the holiday meal.

- Borrow chairs from your church or fellowship hall (Be *sure* to return them!)

- TV trays all around will work if your space is very limited or chopped into small areas.

WELCOMING WEARY TRAVELERS

- Leave the porch light burning and a welcome sign on the door!

- Have beds made and ready for their arrival.

- Have a quick, warm snack waiting for the wayfarers.

- Put towels and washcloths on the foot of the bed—ready for a welcome freshening up for your travelers.

- A warm drink on a cold night of traveling is a great greeting. Avoid caffeine though, unless requested!

- Give your guest the opportunity to rest before you visit.

- Be prepared for babies or pets who may have been on the road too long too!

- Tie ribbons, balloons, or signs to direct travelers to your home if you live in a more remote area.

- Make sure the temperatures of the sleeping areas are set before arrival.

- Warm hugs and smiles are greatly appreciated when greeting weary travelers!

- Make sure dark pathways are well lit before your guests arrive.

- A night-light in the bathroom and hallways is a considerate touch.

HOW TO DIVIDE YOUR HOLIDAY TIME BETWEEN FAMILIES!

❄ Remember, no matter what anyone thinks, you must protect your time with your own immediate family first!

❄ Try Christmas every other year with each family.

❄ Schedule the weekend before or after Christmas to spend the holidays with both sets of family.

❄ Unite those families! Have Christmas all together in one large hall or fellowship room! Why not?

❄ Schedule Christmas in shifts. One family comes in the morning, the other in the afternoon or evening.

❄ Christmas in one place and New Year's/Christmas in the other.

❄ Christmas in July! If you see family only on summer vacation, go ahead and do Christmas in July with them!

❄ Whatever you do, don't divide your family. It is usually a mistake to send some in one direction and the rest in another. Stay together for this special holiday!

❄ Progressive Christmasing will allow you to visit several homes and still stay together as a family. Start with Christmas Eve at one house, breakfast at another, lunch on down the line, and end with your own.

❄ If all else fails, draw straws!

❄ Visit all the close relatives first, and then pack for the longer trip last.

❄ If your children need to go to Dad's house for Christmas make sure you don't put undue stress on them with side comments or facial expressions. Remember, this is the season of love and giving.

HOW TO KEEP YOUR KIDS ENTERTAINED ON THAT HOLIDAY TRIP!

- Prepare a "Fun Box" with small, car-safe toys inside. Get out one toy at a time and space them out over the duration of the trip!

- Blast from the past...Rubics Cubes and Etch-a-Sketch are oldies but goodies! Fun and self contained!

- IPOD, Walkman, CD player and if you are of the SUV generation...pick up some videos for the car...Don't forget those headphones!

- Game Boys and hand held videos are great too.

- Picture books

- Sing it Daddy! Bring sing-along tapes for the whole family and make your trip memorable and fun.

- Sew Fun cardboard lacing cards are great fun and easy to do in a vehicle.

- Got a laptop your teen can be trusted with?

- Some art sets can be used in the car or on a plane...no paint or permanent markers though!

- My word! Word puzzles, vocabulary cards, and word games.

- Origami is a safe and quiet pasttime!

- Felt boards with felts are great...not too many pieces though!

- Oh You little doll! Barbie, Ken, G.I. Joe, and the rest of the dress-up dolls are a good option to keep little hands busy.

- Little girls will play mommy to a baby doll and change those diapers over and over while you drive!

"ARE WE THERE YET?"—GAMES YOU CAN PLAY ON THE ROAD!

I Spy:

* The person who is "IT" looks around inside the car and chooses an object, then says "I spy with my little eye something..."and gives a clue like a color or shape. The other game players try to guess what the person saw. The first one to guess wins and is "IT."

I Am Going out West:

* Each player says in turn "I am going out west, and I am going to take..."and they choose one object...like a horse, a blanket, or even a dill pickle! When each person has chosen an object, the first player says "I am going out West and I am going to take (names his object and what he is going to do with his object) a horse and I am going to ride my horse." The second player and on around the circle have to say the same thing only inserting their object. "I am going to ride my blanket." "I am going to ride my dill pickle." The laughter gets louder as players must say ridiculous lines concerning their object. "I am going out west and I am going to take a pickle and eat it..."then others have to follow suit. "I am going to eat my horse," "I am going to eat my blanket," etc. Fun for the whole family all the way out West...or wherever!

Car Currency:

* Each child chooses a color or type of car and keeps track of how many they see in a 10- or 20-mile length of the trip. The one who chooses wisest and counts the most wins!

Name Game:

❄ Start with the first letter of the alphabet and go around to each player who has to give a boy's or a girl's name corresponding to the letter you are on. Some are simple; some are very hard. Watch for those creative types who make names up. We used the rule if it was a very unusual name no one had heard of, you had to know someone by that name.

My Side Your Side Big Time Landowners:

❄ My mother never liked this game...but my brother and I played it relentlessly just the same!

❄ Two kids in the car on either side. Whatever is on one side of the car that child "owns" and whatever is on the other side the other child "owns." Whoever has accumulated the most buildings or attractions by the end of the trip wins. Beware little sisters: your brother may pull the "Oh we turned; now everything you had is on my side now!"

Tell Me about Heaven:

❄ My dad used to start a game about Heaven to keep our minds in loftier places than they had a tendency to be in on long car trips.

❄ "What do you think Heaven will be like?" he would start out. Then he would say something about Heaven from the Bible. Each of us would get a turn naming or describing what we thought might be in Heaven. This leads to many funny observations and good teaching opportunities.

Don't Let It Be a Blue Christmas

WHEN THE KIDDOS ARE AWAY...

- If your kids are going to be away at Christmas time, fill their suitcases and clothes with little treats and love notes from you. Keep it cheery.

- Begin sending letters a week in advance so that they will receive letters from you every day they are away. This is especially helpful for little ones who are apt to get homesick.

- Give them a cell phone so you can stay in touch. It is important to avoid getting overly melancholy. Smile when you are talking with them. Let them hear the happiness in your voice.

- Exchange journals! Encourage your children to journal while they are away, and you do the same. When they return, you can sit down, trade journals, and talk about all the FUN and new things you each did.

- Send your children off with a disposable camera ...so they can record their adventures!

- Send them off with preaddressed and stamped return envelopes. Fold up cool stationery inside, and you can add prompts for younger children to fill in the blanks.

- Send a letter ahead from the family pet. If you have a picture, include it. You could even have the pet share some exciting or outrageous adventure he is on himself!

- Send a tape of bedtime stories or songs or stories about your childhood along with a tape set and headphones. This is especially helpful if a long journey by car is anticipated.

88

WHEN FAMILY CAN'T COME HOME

Create a family video/Do a skit. (Have your kids act out their latest accomplishments—such as showing off trophies and awards or athletic feats. Sing carols or add personalized messages. Include the family pet...having them perform tricks—don't forget the bow!)

Send a care package complete with a mini tree, treats, colorful drawings, and maybe a Christmas CD.

Send a family portrait—for fun you could add a space or caricature of the missing family member.

Segment some time in the festivities to call those who couldn't be there. Pass the phone around and let everyone take part. This can be especially fun if you have a speaker phone— opening the call with, "We Wish You a Merry Christmas!" (see caroling section page 156.)

Plan ahead and send a delivery or courier balloons, a wreath, or treats on Christmas Day or the day before.

Use the conference call system on your phone to get together with family in different places.

🍪 Send a small package or letter every day for a week before Christmas to keep those reminders coming in!

🍪 Write a letter and have everyone in the family and several of their friends write and tape in cartoons and current events.

🍪 Have a Christmas greeting printed in the hometown newspaper and mail it to your out-of-pocket pal.

🍪 Scan photos of Christmases past and send fun and happy memories across the miles.

🍪 Send a favorite old teddy bear or memento from days gone by in your gift package.

🍪 Make a "WE CARE" package and include little items from several family members or friends that will bring a little holiday cheer.

🍪 Gather a large box full of cards, letters, pictures, and postcards and send a "wealth of prizes."

🍪 Video tape the town, school, workplace, church, and some of the town's people sending their greetings far away.

🍪 Get on the computer and instant message!

🍪 Hop a plane the last minute, if you can, and just show up!

ALONE FOR THE HOLIDAYS

Listen to joyful Christmas music!

Don't feel up to decorating? Try hanging a pretty wreath over the fireplace. It will bring a wonderful smell to your home and is easy to clean up.

Uncle Beauford sent you a Christmas card? Great! Pin it up and leave it open so you can read it more than once. There are good messages in most of those cards, you know!

If you are stationed in a different country, find out all about their traditions for Christmas and write letters explaining them to your family and friends back home.

Have some time on your hands? Write a letter to someone you have never written to in your family. Use red and green pens if you want to. Draw funny facial expressions in between the lines. That ought to put some joy in their Noel!

Invite another friend or two over who can't go home and celebrate together!

Bake or buy some cookies, put them in a pretty container, and give to people who must work Christmas such as policemen, firefighters, and hospital personnel.

Separated from your family for all or part of Christmas? Try reaching out to others and make a positive change in your holiday routine...serve dinner at a homeless shelter. If you have free weekend, holiday, and evening minutes on your cell phone...why not share those treasured minutes and let a few homeless people make a call to loved ones?

Hospitals and children's wards can be a sad place during the holidays. Why not put on a Santa cap and visit a hospital. Have the patients join you in Christmas carols. If you are able, stop by a dollar store on the way for affordable toys or gifts.

Plan ahead and visit a nursing home. You can pass out Christmas cards or gather up a few friends to go caroling with you up and down the hallways. If you are a crafty person, arrange in advance to set up a craft room to make easy projects. Bring Christmas music with you and serve small cups of hot cider. You will no doubt brighten a corner of many lonely hearts.

Why not have Christmas at your house and invite over an "adopted family." Just because you can't go home doesn't mean you can't celebrate the holiday in a meaningful way. Try inviting over young college students who may not be able to get home, a new family from your church, or an elderly person who may have recently lost a spouse. You can make the holiday special for others by opening up your heart and your home.

All Dressed Up and Some Place to Go!

GO FROM OFFICE TO OFFICE PARTY WITH ACCESSORIES

🎄 The Simple Black Dress! Change shoes, add a scarf or jewelry, and you are the hit of the office party!

🎄 Guys, after a quick shave in the men's room, change shoes and tie, splash a little cologne on, and you are set.

🎄 Ladies, pull your hair up and add a festive hair accessory to make your entrance more exciting after work.

🎄 Add a velvet shawl or jacket to your plain working dress or slacks, and you are transformed from day to evening wear with a few glitzes.

🎄 If your office party is casual, remove your tie and bring a Christmas sweater to pull over to "dress down" for the occasion.

🎄 Casual Party? Be the life of the party by wearing deer antlers, jingle bells, or even a light up nose!

🎄 Ladies, a lace shawl usually does it all...tie it around your hips or shoulders.

🎄 Sparkle! Match a hair clip, pin, and shoe clips to quickly transform a look.

HOLIDAY DO DA! FESTIVE HOLIDAY HAIRSTYLES

- A quick ponytail with a festive bow or jingle bells

- Headbands! There are many sparkly, velvety, ribbon-covered headbands you can use to add pizzazz to your holiday look.

- Oh, go ahead! Go for the TIARA! They are sparkly, fun, and very in this year!

- Curl your hair with small, tight curlers, put up in a high ponytail, and fluff for a quick and fancy do.

- Spray in a little glitter! The shine and sparkle will spruce up even the mousiest hair!

- Gel, mousse, and tip with frost or glitter for short hair.

- Add streaks or highlights for a holiday dazzle.

- Use a party rinse that will wash out for a temporary new look.

- Beads, bells, ribbons and more! Braid them in!

PRACTICAL AND HOLIDAY "WHAT TO WEAR" IDEAS!

 Layer it on, Baby! Dress in layers so you can stay comfortable indoors or out.

 Shoes! Keep your tootsies dry and comfy for extra shopping hours—how about carrying an extra pair in the trunk just in case!

 Again when in doubt, the simple black dress will take you where you want to go!

 Pin bells and bows on sweaters and pullovers for an added flair.

 Holiday nails. Why not? Nail art is affordable and available at salons and most malls.

 Don't throw that heavy bag over your shoulder while shopping. Pull out the bare essentials and lighten your load!

 Warm and cozy hats solve a bad hair day in a jiffy! They can also be cute with funny accessories.

 Wear a sweatshirt with ribbons sewn all over it that candy canes can be tied to. You will look fun and festive, and you can give candy canes away to crying kids at the mall or in line!

 The best thing you can wear at Christmas time is a warm and loving smile...even in that long waiting line!

Seasons
Greetings

SEASONAL SENTIMENTS: WHO, WHAT, WHEN, AND HOW TO SEND HOLIDAY MAIL

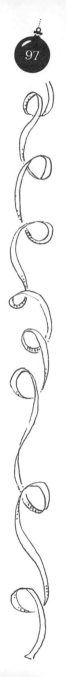

All packages going overseas should be mailed in November or sooner.

Packages mailed in the U.S. should go out as close to December 1st as possible.

Cards and letters should be ready to be mailed the first week of December.

Local card mail should be sent the second week of December.

For glass and delicate items it may be worth it to have a professional packing establishment pack and insure it for delivery.

CREATIVE CHRISTMAS CARDS

- Send a Christmas card from the family pet. You can stamp the paw or draw a paw print and sign the pet's name in crayon—if you really want to be creative.

- Send a family newsletter. For fun ideas on how to, see page 99.

- Fill your cards with holiday confetti!

- Enclose pictures with captions.

- Have your children make their own Christmas cards. Have them include homemade snowflakes. Always a family hit!

HOW TO WRITE A CHRISTMAS NEWSLETTER

🎄 Make your list and check it twice. Are your addresses up to date?

🎄 Save time by writing on the computer...I love spell check!

🎄 Choose a fun font that is easily read.

🎄 Try to "Brighten the Corner Where You Are!" Keep the bad news to a minimum.

🎄 If you had a great year, be sure to mention God's blessings, but don't go on and on. Be sensitive to the fact that the year may have been harder for others.

🎄 Be sure to mention each family member of your household in your yearly highlights.

🎄 Be sure to share about accomplishments, sports, hobbies, and new endeavors.

🎄 You can mention your pets, but most people will not be interested in long recourses about them.

🎄 Buy or create your own Christmas paper to print your letters on.

🎄 Fill your letter with Christmas Confetti!

🎄 Add some humor! Include an appropriate cartoon or short anecdote!

FUN SEASON'S GREETINGS:

Answering Machine Messages

Hi, we're getting ready for Christmas! Leave your name and number and we'll get back with you!

If you are a Shepherd: bless you, and stay warm until we can return your call. If you are the local snowman: be cool! If you are Santa Claus: COME RIGHT ON OVER!!! The rest of you know what to do!

Twas the night before Christmas and all through the house, paper and debris were scattered about. I hear the phone ringing, but I just can't find the silly thing! Leave your name and number, and we'll try to give you a ring!

Hello, I'd answer the phone myself, but I would have to put down my hot cocoa and disturb the sleeping kitty on my lap. When the cookies are done, the buzzer will sound...I will wake up from this dream and call you right back!

Ha ha ha! (laughing) You didn't really think you would catch us at home during this season, did you? Leave your name and number, and we'll call you right back...or come on over, and we'll throw snowballs at you!

Hello, you almost reached the Jones family. We are spending as much time as we can enjoying the holiday together. We will call you back if you really need us to though! Leave a message!

[Have your children sing] "We wish you a Merry Christmas, We wish you a Merry Christmas, We wish you a Merry Christmas, and a Happy New Year!" [Then say] "Leave your message at the tone...Happy Holidays!"

Creative
Christmas
Crafts

CINNAMON APPLESAUCE ORNAMENTS

Fragrant and Fun!

1 cup applesauce

1 cup cinnamon
(available at dollar stores for much less than grocery stores!)

 Mix equal parts of cinnamon and applesauce to make dough.

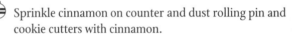 Sprinkle cinnamon on counter and dust rolling pin and cookie cutters with cinnamon.

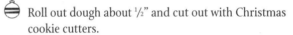 Roll out dough about ½" and cut out with Christmas cookie cutters.

Be sure to make a hole in the top of each "cookie" with a straw so the ornaments can be hung with ribbon when finished.

Bake at 250° for about an hour. Don't burn, but bake thoroughly.

Cool "cookies" and paint with acrylic or tempera paint and trim with puffy white or "snow paint" from the craft store.

When dry, tie a ribbon through the hole and hang your fragrant ornament on the tree, trim a package, or give as a gift. Make sure you let everyone know they are not for eating!

PRETZEL WREATH

Take packaged pretzels and lay them in a circle, side by side, with the small end of the pretzels making the inner circle.

Hot glue sides.

Weave a ribbon in and out of the holes and tie a bow at the top.

You can strengthen the wreath by double siding it.

This makes a great gift, it's fun and easy to make, and any size of pretzel can be used!

THE CHRISTMAS CANDY CANE STORY

Long ago, a candy maker wanted to make a piece of candy that would remind his customers to celebrate Jesus at Christmas. He created the candy cane as his special gift to the Lord.

The candy maker started with a white piece of candy that stood for the purity of the Lord.

He shaped it like a "J" for Jesus. When he turned it upside down he saw it became the staff of his shepherd.

The red stripes would remind everyone of the cost of their salvation that comes through Jesus' blood.

He added the peppermint flavor to symbolize the spices which were gifts from the wise men.

Today this simple candy still reminds us to celebrate the sweetest gift of Christmas—Jesus!

ICE CREAM CONE ORNAMENTS

Package of sugar cones

Tissue paper in pastel "ice cream" colors

Package of 4" Styrofoam balls

Package of clear, large crystal glitter
  (Looks like ice cream sprinkles!)

White glue

Paintbrush

Small hook or loop of ribbon

 Take the ice cream cones and paint them inside and out with glue and let them dry.

 Glue a Styrofoam ball onto each cone.

 Tear tissue paper into 1- 1½ inch squares.

 Paint Styrofoam ball with glue and cover with tissue paper squares, overlapping with at least three layers.

 Sprinkle top of cone with crystals and let dry.

 Put small hook in top of cone or hot glue a ribbon loop to the back so they can be hung on the tree!

CANDY CANE CRAFT FOR LITTLE FINGERS

Red and white chenille stems (pipe cleaners)
Green ribbon
Wire cutters or old scissors

Take the chenille stems and cut them in half.

Make a tiny bend in the top and bottoms to keep little ones from getting poked by wire.

Show your child how to twist the stems evenly to look like candy canes.

Bend the tops over and add a bright green bow.

They are ready to hang on the tree, put on a package, or decorate a wreath! This is a real kid pleaser, I promise!

You can also take two candy canes and hot glue them crossed in the middle and add a bow to the center to make a holiday pin or larger decoration.

YOU ARE ALL HEART!

Box of candy canes
Hot glue gun
Holiday sequins
Bow

 Take 2 candy canes at a time and put them together to form a heart shape.

 Hot glue top and bottom where they meet.

 Cover glued area with a small holiday sequin.

 Alternate the hearts right side up, then right side down in a wreath circle.

 Hot glue circle together.

 Add a holiday bow, and you have a sweet wreath!

 (Hot Glue Guns are NOT for kids! This is a project for YOU!)

THE SNOW GLOBE

Baby food jar or clear jar with tight-fitting lid
Silver, gold, or white glitter
Small plastic Christmas toy or ornament
Water
Hot Glue
(Optional) Spray paint, colored tape, or contact paper

Take the lid of your jar and spray paint it or cover it with colored tape or contact paper if you wish.

Hot glue a small plastic toy or Christmas ornament to the INSIDE of the lid.

Pour glitter into the jar.

Fill with water to the very brim.

Place a ring of hot glue around the INSIDE of the jar lid and quickly screw it on the jar of water.

When the glue cools, turn your jar over and watch the glittery "snow" fly!

SOCK IT TO ME SNOWMAN!

Men's white tube sock

Tissue paper or newspaper

Rubber bands

Permanent marker in green, red, black

Small piece of cardboard

1 "bumpy style" chenille stem (pipe cleaner)

Black sequins

Cut 5-6" off of the top of the sock band and lay aside for scarf and cap.

 Head:

Stuff the toe of the sock with a ball of paper for the snowman's head.

Wrap a rubber band around it to hold it in place.

 Body:

Stuff a larger amount of paper in the sock to form a large egg-shaped body.

Cut the cardboard to make a round base to help the snowman stand.

Insert cardboard.

Hot glue the ends of the sock across bottom.

Scrunch and adjust snowman until he can "stand" solidly on base.

Scarf:

Take scissors and cut 1 inch off sock band.

Cut this band so it will lay out flat.

Use red or green permanent markers to make striped "scarf" for snowman.

You can fringe the ends and wrap it around his neck.

Cap:

Use the rest of the 4 or 5 inches from sock band for a "knitted cap."

Wrap a rubber band around one end leaving enough room to fringe the top to look like a pom-pom.

Use red or green marker to stripe the cap.

Pull the cap down over the snowman's head.

Face:

Use black sequins for eyes and "coal" smile.

Cut one of the "bumps" from the orange chenille stem. It will look a lot like a carrot!

Carefully put hot glue on the wide end and glue to the center of the snowman's face.

Ta Da! You have an adorable and inexpensive decoration, gift, or wreath ornament. (My school kids sold these for $3.50 apiece to raise money for the Art Club! We sold about 100 of them!)

FRAGRANT DOOR OR HALLWAY SACHET

These make nice and inexpensive gifts you or your kids can make!

Yarn colors of your choice...match your home or use Christmas colors

$\frac{1}{4}$" or $\frac{1}{2}$" cloth ribbon

1-2" brass or silver colored ring

Cinnamon sticks

Small silk flowers (optional)

 Take several lengths of yarn 3-4' long (the more lengths the thicker the braid.)

 Pull the yarn halfway through the ring and even up the ends.

 Braid the yarn in a neat but soft braid.

 Tie with ribbon at the bottom.

 Tie three to five 6" lengths of ribbon evenly spaced down the braid.

 Tie three cinnamon sticks to each ribbon.

 Insert silk flowers, if you choose, in between the cinnamon stick bunches.

 This braid can be hung on the door, in the hall or bathroom or in closets to make them smell cinnamony good.

 You can substitute with jingle bells, small ornaments, or whatever you like to change the look of your door sachet.

DO IT IN DOUGH!

These are fun to make, easy to sell, and fun to receive!

Buy Crayola Model Magic, Sculpy, Fimo, or any other air-dry or baking dough you choose to make wonderful handmade ornaments and pins to wear or decorate your tree, packages, or refrigerators with!

Make your own dough:

Mix 2 cups of flour with 1 cup of salt and add about 1 cup of water until dough is workable. Flour your rolling pin and cookie cutters and cut out like regular cookies. Bake at 250° for about an hour and a half and cool. Dough should be very hard and ready to decorate or paint when cool.

Take your dough, and be sure you read and follow directions on package.

Roll out your dough.

Cut with regular or your favorite tiny cookie cutters.

Don't forget to make a hole in the top if you are going to hang your decorations!

Dry or bake the dough as directed.

Paint the ornaments with acrylic or tempera paints and glitter them too if you like!

You can a hang them on a tree, decorate packages with them, hot glue a pin back on them to wear, or attach a magnet to the back side for refrigerator art.

PLENTY OF PINE CONES!

From the tiniest little cones to the enormous redwood and Douglas fir cones, pine cones are plentiful and popular! Here are some ideas for your decorating and gift-giving needs:

- A large bowl or glass fish bowl filled with natural colored pine cones and small Christmas balls make a beautiful centerpiece.

- Tiny pine cones can be tied or hot glued with ribbons and worn as pins.

- Spray painting or frosting pine cones with gold or silver glitter can revive old and gray cones for new decorating ideas.

- Fill up baskets with pine cones and put bows on them for your porch, fireplace, or table.

- Take a paintbrush and lightly paint the tips of the cones with white paint and/or glitter to add sparkle to your projects with cones.

- Kids love to stand them upright, paint them green, and decorate them with beads and sequins to look like miniature Christmas trees.

- Hot glue the ends of three good-sized pine cones to 2" ribbon and let them hang at different lengths with a large bow above them for door décor.

- Join them with wire into a wreath shape and leave natural or paint green, gold, or silver. Accent with bows, balls, or bells for a front door wreath.

- Use them as accents for your gift baskets.

- Use small ones or cut larger ones down and add to your own potpourri.

- Decorate gifts with pine cones tied on with ribbon or raffia.

- Cut off the tops or the bottoms so they will stand, and add a small wooden candleholder and candle to the top.

- Wire them to your green garland to make it look more woodsy or realistic.

- Glue them together into a triangular cone shape and decorate as a small Christmas tree.

THE SHAM SCAM! CHEAP AND SWEET HOLIDAY PILLOW COVERS

Love those beautiful Christmas pillows you see in fine stores everywhere, but don't have the money or the space to store them? Here's a thought...

 Measure the throw pillows you already have and go buy enough holiday fabric to cover them! Go ahead and get fancy and add some fun trims too.

 After you have measured your pillows, cut your fabric slightly larger than your pillow.

 Pin lace or trims to the right side of the fabric facing IN to the first piece of fabric.

 Pin the right side of the second piece facing the right side of the first.

 Stitch all around leaving one side open.

 Pull the new cover over your old pillow and baste it closed for easy removal after Christmas.

 You can use these pillow slips to brighten your home year after year and not have the expense or storage problem after the holiday!

 Naturally, you could permanently change your pillows, or take the stuffing out of old pillows for your new ones.

Cookin' Up
Christmas!

SUGAR-FREE, LOW-CARB, AND OTHER TREATS YOU CAN SERVE FOR CHRISTMAS

- Jigglin' Jingle Bells! Sugar Free Jell-O shapes (see package for details). Use cookie cutter shapes.

- Splendid Sugarless Cookies! Substitute Splenda sugar substitute in all your cookie recipes!

- Cut veggies in fun shapes and fill with low-fat cream cheese.

- Use wraps instead of breads when making finger sandwiches.

- Use turkey ham and chicken with veggies when making toothpick hors d'oeuvres. They are yummy and low fat.

- Dream Date: Fill dates with low fat cream cheese and push a walnut half inside for a very tasty and nutritious finger food.

- Spike the Punch? Sure! Use sugar substitute in your favorite holiday punches, or substitute Crystal Light for a fun flavored drink.

- Sweets for the Sweet: Fill your candy dishes with trail mixes and sprinkle just a few chocolate chips in the mix.

- Veggie and fruit plates go over big during the holidays when everyone has had so many sweets and baked goods everywhere else.

- Flavored teas served hot or cold are a low calorie hit for holiday parties.

- A little dab of sugarfree whipped topping on low carb cookies and fruit bars dress them up for any holiday table and are a guilt free little treat for all who are watching their weight!

PARTY PUNCH RECIPES

HOT 18TH CENTURY DRINK

1 quart sweet apple cider

12 whole cloves

5 cinnamon sticks

1 (4 oz.) pkg. Red Hot cinnamon candies

Combine all ingredients in a saucepan.

Mix well.

Simmer for 15 minutes.

Ladle into mugs.

Makes 4 Cups.

 DUSTY ROSE PUNCH

1 large can pineapple juice (46 oz.)

1 small can frozen pink lemonade, thawed (6 oz.)

1 quart raspberry sherbet, softened

2 quarts ginger ale, chilled.

Blend pineapple juice and lemonade in punch bowl.

Stir in sherbet.

Add ginger ale just before serving.

Makes 25 servings.

NOTE: This is a very pretty punch to serve at Christmas time.

HOT SPICED PUNCH

2 cinnamon sticks

1 1/2 cups sugar

1 1/2 cups water

1/2 cup Red Hot cinnamon candies

1/2 cup honey

1 large can pineapple juice (46 oz.)

1 large can orange juice (46 oz.)

1 pint strong tea

Tie cinnamon sticks in cheesecloth.

Combine sugar, water, and candies in saucepan.

Add cinnamon sticks.

Simmer for 30 minutes or until candies are melted.

Remove cinnamon sticks.

Stir in honey, pineapple juice, and orange juice.

Put into large container and let stand overnight.

Stir in tea, and reheat before serving.

May be served cold if you prefer.

STRAWBERRY BANANA CRUSH

4 small packages unsweetened Kool-Aid

4 cups sugar

1 large can pineapple juice (46 oz.)

2 (10 oz.) Pkgs. frozen strawberries, thawed

6 bananas, mashed

1 quart 7-Up

Combine drink mix, sugar, and pineapple juice in large freezer container.

Mix well.

Stir in strawberries, bananas, and 7-up.

Freeze until slushy, stirring occasionally.

Makes 16 cups.

 WASSAIL

2 quarts sweet apple cider   1 cup sugar

2 cups orange juice   1 cinnamon stick

1 cup lemon juice   1 tsp. whole cloves

5 cups pineapple juice

Combine all ingredients in saucepan and bring just to a boil.

Remove from heat and strain to remove spices.

Serve hot.

Makes approx. 16 Cups.

 EASY BANANA PUNCH

4 bananas

1 (12 oz.) can frozen orange juice

2 cups sugar

1 large can pineapple juice

2 quarts ginger ale

6 cups water

Combine bananas and small amount of orange juice in blender.

Blend until smooth.

Mix together all ingredients except ginger ale in a freezer container.

Freeze until ready to use.

Thaw until slushy and add ginger ale just before serving time.

Makes 5 quarts.

SWEETS & TREATS

ICE CREAM CAKE CONES

These are incredibly easy and make a fun, festive presentation.

Take standard cake cones and fill them with cake batter, just as you would a cupcake.

You will want to fill them just a tiny bit past the halfway mark.

Place them in a cake pan, side by side.

It is best to fill your cake pan up with extra cones so they don't all topple over.

Bake with the cupcake guidelines on your cake mix.

The cake will rise and round.

Once baked, allow them to cool.

Frost and top with a cherry, and it looks just like an ice cream cone.

What's better, you don't need a plate!

BANANA BREAD

*Delicious and freezes well so you can prepare ahead
for guests, mailing, or gift giving!*

½ cup shortening	1 cup sugar

Cream these two together.

2 eggs, well beaten	1 teaspoon salt
4 ripe bananas mashed	½ cup chopped nuts
2 cups sifted flour	1 teaspoon vanilla

Mix in order given.

Bake at 350° in greased loaf pans for approximately 30 minutes.

Makes 5 baby loaves.

 CRANBERRY SQUARES

Looks delicious and tastes even better!

½ cup shortening

1 cup brown sugar

1½ cups flour

1 teaspoon soda

½ teaspoon salt

1½ cups uncooked oats

1 can cranberry sauce (whole berry style)

Cream shortening and sugar together in another bowl.

Mix flour, soda, salt, and oats.

Crumble together with sugar mixture.

Press half of this FIRMLY into 13"x9"x2" pan.

Spread cranberry sauce evenly over this.

Add remainder of crumb mixture and press lightly.

Bake at 350° for 30 minutes.

Cool, cut, and enjoy!

MMM! MAGIC COOKIE BARS

These can also be prepared ahead and frozen. They make great gifts too!

$\frac{1}{2}$ cup margarine

1$\frac{1}{2}$ cups vanilla wafer crumbs

1 cup chopped walnuts

1 cup (6 oz.) chocolate chips

1$\frac{1}{3}$ cups coconut

1$\frac{1}{3}$ cups (15 oz. can) Eagle Brand milk

Pour melted butter into bottom of 13"x9"x2" pan.

Sprinkle cookie crumbs over melted butter.

Sprinkle chopped nuts over crumbs.

Press down gently.

Scatter chocolate chips over nuts. Sprinkle coconut on.

Pour condensed milk evenly over coconut.

Bake at 350° for 25 minutes or until LIGHTLY browned on top.

Cool in pan for 15 minutes.

Cut into bars, eat, and slip off to holiday heaven!

KIDS' COOKIE CUTTER FAVORITES!

ROLL OUT LEMON COOKIES

These are great for Christmas cookies to cut out and decorate!
They will freeze well baked or decorated if you freeze on a
sheet before you stack them. These can be used to put personal
names on for gifts too!

3 cups flour	1 cup soft margarine
1½ teaspoon baking powder	1 egg, beaten
½ teaspoon salt	1 teaspoon vanilla
1 cup sugar	

Lemon flavoring as desired, or other light flavoring!

Cream or canned milk as needed to make dough workable.

Cream sugar, margarine, and egg together.

Add all other ingredients, except the flour.

Cream the dough as you pour in the flour, small amounts at
a time.

Chill for 15 minutes.

Roll out ½ inch thickness and cut with floured cookie cutters.

Bake at 350° 7-9 minutes until lightly browned on the
bottom edges.

 SHORTBREAD STARS

Old-fashioned favorite and freezable!

1 cup butter or margarine   ½ cup sugar

2 ½ cups sifted flour

Cream butter and sugar until light and fluffy.

Stir in flour until smooth; dough will be stiff.

Refrigerate for several hours until ready to roll out.

Roll out on floured surface ⅓ inch thickness and cut with star cookie cutters.

Place on ungreased cookie sheet.

Bake at 300° until golden brown. Cool on wire rack.

CRUNCHY PEANUT BALLS

1 cup sugar	1 teaspoon vanilla
1 cup light cream or canned milk, undiluted	5 cups corn or wheat flakes
	2 cups crispy rice cereal
1 cup light corn syrup	1 cup salted peanuts

In medium saucepan, combine sugar, cream, and corn syrup.

Cook over low heat, stirring until sugar is dissolved.

Continue cooking until candy thermometer reads "softball" stage.

Add vanilla.

While this is cooking, in a large, buttered bowl combine cornflakes, rice cereal, and peanuts; toss to mix well.

Add cooked syrup. Mix thoroughly.

Refrigerate 30 minutes.

With buttered hands, form 1½ inch balls.

Makes about 48.

CHOCOLATE FONDUE

2 packages (6 oz. size) semi-sweet chocolate chips

1 can (13 oz.) evaporated milk, undiluted

$\frac{1}{2}$ cup orange juice

1 tablespoon grated orange peel

In heavy saucepan, combine chocolate and milk.

Cook over low heat, stirring constantly, until chocolate is melted.

Stir in juice and orange peel.

Remove from heat.

Serve warm in fondue pot, surrounded by fruit and/or cake for dipping.

Makes 6-8 servings.

Fruit options for dipping: apple slices, orange or tangerine sections, dates, seedless grapes, pineapple chunks, marshmallows, squares of angel food cake, vanilla wafers.

QUICK CASSEROLES FOR BUSY HOLIDAYS!

 CHICKEN AND RICE

Tastes great, easy to serve or carry to a get-together and freezes well also.

3 chicken breasts (cut in bite sizes if desired)

$\frac{1}{2}$ cup margarine

1 can cream of chicken soup

$2\frac{1}{2}$ tablespoons finely chopped parsley

1 teaspoon salt

dash of black pepper

$1\frac{1}{3}$ cups minute rice

$1\frac{1}{3}$ cups water

Roll chicken in flour and brown lightly in margarine (low heat).

Remove chicken and stir soup, seasonings, and water into the drippings.

Bring to a boil.

Spread minute rice (uncooked) into a $1\frac{1}{2}$ quart shallow casserole dish.

Pour all but $\frac{1}{2}$ or so of soup mixture over rice and stir until well moistened.

Press chicken pieces down into rice and pour on the rest of the soup.

Cover tightly with foil.

Bake at 375° for 40 minutes.

🎄 CHUCK WAGON BEAN ROAST

Make the night before or in a crock pot while you are out!

¹/₃ pound chuck roast

1 pound bag pinto beans, rinsed

1, 7-ounce can chopped green chilies

1, 8-ounce can Rotel tomato sauce

1 large onion, thinly sliced

¹/₄ - ¹/₂ teaspoon garlic salt

Place roast and beans in Dutch oven (large, covered, oven-safe pan).

Add water to cover.

Add all other ingredients.

Cover and bake at 250° for 12 hours.

ORIENTAL HAMBURGER HASH

Tastes way better than it sounds and serves a BIG GROUP!
(Can be frozen)

1 pound ground beef

2 medium onions, chopped

1 cup sliced celery

1 can cream of mushroom soup

1 can cream of chicken soup

1 ½ cups warm water

1 ½ cups minute rice, uncooked

½ cup soy sauce

½ teaspoon pepper

1 can bean sprouts, drained and rinsed

1 can water chestnuts, sliced

1 teaspoon salt

1 large can chow mein noodles

Brown beef and onions.

Add all other ingredients except ½ of the chow mein noodles.

Mix well.

Pour into large casserole dish.

Top with remaining chow mein noodles.

Bake at 350° for 40 minutes.

Serve with additional chow mein noodles and soy sauce
if desired.

🎄 CORN CASSEROLE

1 can whole kernel corn, drained

1 can cream style corn

1 stick melted butter or margarine

8 ounces sour cream

2 eggs, slightly beaten

1 package cornbread mix (8 oz.)

1 cup milk

2 cups grated cheddar cheese

Mix all ingredients except cheddar cheese.

Bake in shallow casserole dish at 350° for 20 minutes.

Put cheese on top and bake 10 minutes more.

Serve warm. Yummy to the tummy!

MEXICAN CHICKEN CASSEROLE

4 chicken breasts

1 ½ cups grated cheddar cheese

1 can cream of chicken soup

1 can cream of mushroom soup

1 can Rotel tomatoes and chilies

1 medium onion

tortilla chips, broken in small pieces enough
   to make a layer across casserole

Boil the chicken and cut into bite-size pieces. Save 1 cup of
chicken stock.

Sauté the onion in margarine.

Combine the soups and the Rotel tomatoes and chilies.

Add 1 cup of chicken stock and the sautéed onion.

In a 9"x13" dish, layer tortilla chips, chicken, soup mixture,
and grated cheese.

Bake at 350° for approximately ½ hour.

Let's Go Caroling!

AWAY IN A MANAGER

Away in a manger, no crib for a bed,
The little Lord Jesus laid down His sweet head.
The stars in the sky looked down where He lay,
The little Lord Jesus asleep in the hay.

The cattle are lowing, the baby awakes,
But little Lord Jesus no crying He makes.
I love Thee, Lord Jesus, look down from the sky
And stay by my cradle til morning is nigh.

Be near me, Lord Jesus, I ask Thee to stay
Close by me forever, and love me, I pray.
Bless all the dear children in Thy tender care,
And take us to heaven, to live with Thee there.

AUTHOR OF LYRICS FOR VERSES 1-2 UNKNOWN
VERSE 3 ATTRIBUTED TO JOHN THOMAS MCFARLAND
MUSIC BY WILLIAM J. KIRKPATRICK, 1895

HARK! THE HERALD ANGELS SING

Hark! the herald angels sing,
"Glory to the newborn King!
Peace on earth, and mercy mild,
God and sinners reconciled."
Joyful, all ye nations, rise,
Join the triumph of the skies;
With th' angelic host proclaim,
"Christ is born in Bethlehem."
Hark! the herald angels sing,
"Glory to the newborn King!"

Christ, by highest heav'n adored:
Christ, the everlasting Lord;
Late in time behold Him come,
Offspring of the favored one.
Veil'd in flesh, the Godhead see;
Hail, th' incarnate Deity:
Pleased, as man, with men to dwell,

HARK! THE HERALD ANGELS SING (continued)

Jesus, our Emmanuel!
Hark! the herald angels sing,
"Glory to the newborn King!"

Hail! the heav'n-born Prince of Peace!
Hail! the Son of Righteousness!
Light and life to all He brings,
Risen with healing in His wings
Mild He lays His glory by,
Born that man no more may die:
Born to raise the sons of earth,
Born to give them second birth.
Hark! the herald angels sing,
"Glory to the newborn King!"

CHARLES WESLEY, 1739

SILENT NIGHT

Silent night, holy night!
All is calm, all is bright.
Round yon Virgin, Mother and Child.
Holy infant so tender and mild,
Sleep in heavenly peace,
Sleep in heavenly peace.

Silent night, holy night!
Shepherds quake at the sight.
Glories stream from heaven afar
Heavenly hosts sing Alleluia,
Christ the Savior is born!
Christ the Savior is born.

Silent night, holy night!
Son of God, love's pure light.
Radiant beams from Thy holy face
With dawn of redeeming grace,
Jesus Lord, at Thy birth.
Jesus Lord, at Thy birth.

JOSEPH MOHR, 1818

I'M DREAMING OF A WHITE CHRISTMAS

I'm dreaming of a white Christmas
Just like the ones I used to know
Where the treetops glisten
and children listen
To hear sleigh bells in the snow.

I'm dreaming of a white Christmas
With every Christmas card I write
May your days be merry and bright
And may all your Christmases be white.

I'm dreaming of a white Christmas
With every Christmas card I write
May your days be merry and bright
And may all your Christmases be white.

IRVING BERLIN, 1942

OH COME, ALL YE FAITHFUL

O come, all ye faithful,
Joyful and triumphant,
O come ye,
O come ye to Bethlehem;
Come and behold Him
Born the King of angels;
O come, let us adore Him,
O come, let us adore Him,
O come, let us adore Him,
Christ, the Lord.

Sing, choirs of angels,
Sing in exultation,
Sing, all ye citizens
of heaven above;
Glory to God,
Glory in the highest;
O come, let us adore Him,
O come, let us adore Him,
O come, let us adore Him,
Christ, the Lord.

OH COME, ALL YE FAITHFUL (continued)

Yea, Lord, we greet Thee,
Born this happy morning,
Jesus, to Thee be
all glory given;
Son of the Father,
Now in flesh appearing;
O come, let us adore Him,
O come, let us adore Him,
O come, let us adore Him,
Christ, the Lord.

ATTRIBUTED TO JOHN FRANCIS WADE, 1711-1786

WE THREE KINGS OF ORIENT ARE

We three kings of Orient are,
Bearing gifts we traverse afar,
Field and fountain, morr and mountain,
Following yonder Star.

CHORUS
O, star of wonder, star of might,
Star with royal beauty bright,
Westward leading, still proceeding,
Guide us to the perfect light.

Born a babe on Bethlehem's plain;
Gold we bring to crown Him again;
King forever, ceasing never,
Over us all to reign.

*Repeat Chorus *

Frankincense to offer have I;
Incense owns a Deity nigh;
Prayer and praising, all men raising,
Worship Him, God on High.

Repeat Chorus

WE THREE KINGS OF ORIENT ARE (continued)

Myrrh is mine; its bitter perfume
Breathes a life of gathering gloom;
Sorrowing, sighing, bleeding, dying,
Seal'd in the stone-cold tomb.

Repeat Chorus

Glorious now behold Him arise,
King and God and sacrifice,
Heaven sings, "Hallelujah!"
Hallejujah!" Earth replies.

Repeat Chorus

HENRY HOPKINS JR. AUTHOR AND COMPOSER, 1857

JINGLE BELLS

Dashing through the snow,
In a one-horse open sleigh
Through the fields we go, laughing all the way.
Bells on bob-tail ring, making spirits bright
What fun it is to ride and sing,
A sleighing song tonight.

Chorus
Jingle bells, jingle bells, Jingle all the way,
Oh what fun it is to ride in a one-horse open sleigh,
O jingle bells, jingle bells, jingle all the way,
Oh what fun it is to ride in a one-horse open sleigh.

A day or two ago, I thought I'd take a ride
And soon Miss Fanny Bright,
Was seated by my side;
The horse was lean and lank,
Misfortune seemed his lot,
We ran into a drifted bank,
and there we got upset.

Repeat Chorus

JINGLE BELLS (continued)

A day or two ago,
The story I must tell, I went out on the snow
And on my back I fell; a gent was riding by
In a one-horse open sleigh, He laughed at me as
I there sprawling laid, but quickly drove away.

* Repeat Chorus *

JAMES LORD PIERPONT, 1859

RUDOLPH THE RED-NOSED REINDEER

You know Dasher and Dancer
And Prancer and Vixen,
Comet and Cupid
And Donner and Blitzen.
But do you recall
The most famous reindeer of all?

Rudolph the red-nosed reindeer
Had a very shiny nose
And if you ever saw it
You would even say it glows

All of the other reindeer
Used to laugh and call him names
They never let poor Rudolph
Play in any reindeer games

Then one foggy Christmas Eve
Santa came to say
Rudolph with your nose so bright
Won't you guide my sleigh tonight?
Then all the reindeer loved him

RUDOLPH THE RED-NOSED REINDEER
(continued)

And they shouted out with glee
"Rudolph the red-nosed reindeer
You'll go down in history!"

WORDS BY ROBERT L. MAY © 1947
MUSIC BY JOHNNY MARKS

JOY TO THE WORLD

Joy to the world! The Lord is come:
Let earth receive her King.
Let ev'ry heart prepare Him room,
And heaven and nature sing,
And heaven and nature sing,
And heaven and heaven and nature sing.

He rules the world with truth and grace,
And makes the nations prove
The glories of His righteousness
And wonders of His love,
And wonders of His love,
And wonders, wonders of His love.

ISAAC WATTS, 1674-1748

THE TWELVE DAYS OF CHRISTMAS

On the first day of Christmas
my true love sent to me:
A partridge in a pear tree.

On the second day of Christmas
my true love sent to me:
Two turtledoves
And a partridge in a pear tree.

On the third day of Christmas
my true love sent to me:
Three French hens,
Two turtledoves
And a partridge in a pear tree.

On the fourth day of Christmas
my true love sent to me:
Four calling birds,
Three French hens,
Two turtledoves
And a partridge in a pear tree.

THE TWELVE DAYS OF CHRISTMAS (continued)

On the fifth day of Christmas
my true love sent to me:
Five golden rings,
Four calling birds,
Three French hens,
Two turtledoves
And a partridge in a pear tree.

On the sixth day of Christmas
my true love sent to me:
Six geese a laying,
Five golden rings,
Four calling birds,
Three French hens,
Two turtledoves
And a partridge in a pear tree.

On the seventh day of Christmas
my true love sent to me:
Seven swans a swimming,
Six geese a laying,
Five golden rings,
Four calling birds,
Three French hens,
Two turtledoves
And a partridge in a pear tree.

THE TWELVE DAYS OF CHRISTMAS (continued)

On the eighth day of Christmas
my true love sent to me:
Eight maids a milking,
Seven swans a swimming,
Six geese a laying,
Five golden rings,
Four calling birds,
Three French hens,
Two turtledoves
And a partridge in a pear tree.

On the ninth day of Christmas
my true love sent to me:
Nine ladies dancing,
Eight maids a milking,
Seven swans a swimming,
Six geese a laying,
Five golden rings,
Four calling birds,
Three French hens,
Two turtledoves
And a partridge in a pear tree.

THE TWELVE DAYS OF CHRISTMAS (continued)

On the tenth day of Christmas
my true love sent to me:
Ten lords a leaping,
Nine ladies dancing,
Eight maids a milking,
Seven swans a swimming,
Six geese a laying,
Five golden rings,
Four calling birds,
Three French hens,
Two turtledoves
And a partridge in a pear tree.

On the eleventh day of Christmas
my true love sent to me:
Eleven pipers piping,
Ten lords a leaping,
Nine ladies dancing,
Eight maids a milking,
Seven swans a swimming,
Six geese a laying,
Five golden rings,
Four calling birds,
Three French hens,
Two turtledoves
And a partridge in a pear tree.

THE TWELVE DAYS OF CHRISTMAS (continued)

On the twelfth day of Christmas
my true love sent to me:
Twelve drummers drumming,
Eleven pipers piping,
Ten lords a leaping,
Nine ladies dancing,
Eight maids a milking,
Seven swans a swimming,
Six geese a laying,
Five golden rings,
Four calling birds,
Three French hens,
Two turtledoves
And a partridge in a pear tree.

AUTHOR UNKNOWN

IT CAME UPON A MIDNIGHT CLEAR

It came upon the midnight clear,
that glorious song of old.
From angels bending near the earth
to touch their harps of gold.
Peace on the earth, goodwill to men,
from heav'n's all gracious king
The world in solemn stillness lay
to hear the angels sing.

Still through the cloven skies they come
with peaceful wings unfurl
And still their heavenly music floats,
O'er all the weary world.
Above its sad and lowly plains
they bend on hovering wing
And ever o'er its Babel sounds
the blessed angels sing.

IT CAME UPON A MIDNIGHT CLEAR (continued)

O ye, beneath life's crushing load,
whose forms are bending low
Who toil along the climbing way
with painful steps and slow
Look now for glad and golden hours come
swiftly on the wing.
O rest beside the weary road
and hear the angels sing.

For lo the days are hastening on,
by prophets seen of old
When with the ever circling years
shall come the time foretold.
When the new heaven and earth shall own
the Prince of Peace their King
And the whole world send back the song
which now the angels sing.

EDMUND H. SEARS, 1849

WE WISH YOU A MERRY CHRISTMAS

We wish you a merry Christmas
We wish you a merry Christmas
We wish you a merry Christmas
And a happy New Year.
Glad tidings we bring
To you and your kin;
Glad tidings for Christmas
And a happy New Year!

We want some figgy pudding
We want some figgy pudding
We want some figgy pudding
Please bring it right here!
Glad tidings we bring
To you and your kin;
Glad tidings for Christmas
And a happy New Year!

157

WE WISH YOU A MERRY CHRISTMAS (continued)

We won't go until we get some
We won't go until we get some
We won't go until we get some
So bring it out here!
Glad tidings we bring
To you and your kin;
Glad tidings for Christmas
And a happy New Year!

We wish you a Merry Christmas
We wish you a Merry Christmas
We wish you a Merry Christmas
And a happy New Year.
Glad tidings we bring
To you and your kin;
Glad tidings for Christmas
And a happy New Year!

AUTHOR UNKNOWN, BUT SONG IS BELIEVED
TO DATE BACK TO 16TH CENTURY ENGLAND

ABOUT THE AUTHOR

Darla Satterfield Davis, graduated from Southwestern Adventist University in north Texas and is well traveled, an inspiration inherited from her father. She is a gifted artist, has several artistic awards to her credit, and has been teaching the creative arts for many years.

Among her numerous accomplishments, Davis is the recipient of the prestigious "Who's Who of American Teachers Award" and is the owner and founder of The Christian Fine Arts Center in Cleburne, Texas.

Davis has a special love for her volunteer work as a U.S. Citizenship Instructor. In her younger years she had the impressive honor of being Youth Ambassador representing the United States to Europe and was a decathlon winner placing second in the high jump and first in long jump.

She is a contributing writer for several publishing houses and newspapers, and loves to garden. Darla takes great pride in mentoring and investing in the lives of others and is especially close to her daughter, who coincidentally just so happens to be her best friend.

Additional copies of this book
are available from your local bookstore.

Visit our website at:
www.whitestonebooks.com

If you have enjoyed this book
we would love to hear from you.
Please write us at:
White Stone Books
Department E
1501 South Florida Avenue
Lakeland, Florida 33803

WHITE STONE BOOKS
LAKELAND, FLORIDA